_____

_____

All Rights Reserved. No part of this book may be reproduced or transmitted in any form or by any means, electronic, mechanical, photocopying, recording, or otherwise without prior written permission of the publisher and copyright owners.

## Please Read this First

This book is a bridge to your new life!

Do not allow the brevity of each page or the simplicity of the words cause you to treat the use of this book lightly.

**This book is designed to help you save and improve your marriage by way of using text messages.**

If you desire to improve your marriage, this notebook was designed specifically for you.

No matter what level of disconnection and pain your marital relationship is currently experiencing, your marriage can be saved, improved and be a happy one.

This book uses a simple principle and strategy that will help you reconnect with your wife and save or improve your marriage.

The **PRINCIPLE:** Treat a man as his actions deserve, and he will remain as he is – Treat a man as he ought to behave, and he will raise the standard.

**And what does this mean?** Well, if your wife is behaving like an idiot and you respond by treating her like an idiot, she will remain behaving like an idiot. On the other hand, if your wife is behaving like an idiot and you treat her like a queen, she will rise her standard and become the queen.

The **STRATEGY:** Send loving and encouraging text messages to her everyday at the same time for the next 30 days.

# Why These Text Messages?

Love is your wife what respect is to you. Her crave for love is equal your need for respect. When she feels starved of love, its like how you would feel if she disrespects and humiliates you. This text message strategy has been used and proven efficient since the year 2012.

## How it Really Works:
Send your text messages everyday (six days per week) at the same time, preferably in the mornings. 8:30am and 9am have proven to be every effective for most people.

**And What if She Responds?** When she responds, respond back. If she asks why you are sending the messages, answer "because it is true", or do not respond at all.

**And What If The Text Message Is Completely The Opposite Of her Character?** Good question. If for example, the text message of the day says "You are an honest woman", but in reality, she is a liar, the strategy is to treat your wife as she ought to behave and she will raise to the standard. She may in fact be a liar, and your strategy is to help her be the honest woman.

**Do Not** send more than one text message per day. This does not mean that you should not communicate about other things. It just means this intervention strategy should be separate from you other everyday business.

## 9 Things You Should NOT Do During this Phase

1. No matter how much hurt you are, do not ever send her angry text messages.
2. Do not apologize over text message.
3. If you are facing divorce or she has left, do not apologize yet. You can do so in person after you have seen that the two of you are reconnecting. Only after the first 30 days of you sending the text messages.
4. If she is cheating on you or living with someone else, do not send your text message when she might be with the person that she is cheating on you with.
5. For the first two weeks, do not send more than one text message per day. Two will be okay, but do not flood her with your messages. Putting pressure on her may cause her to back-off from you more. I highly recommend that you stick to one text message per day.
6. Most probably on or by the 3rd day, she will call you and ask you what's going on or why you are sending these messages. If she asks you why, you could say; "because it is true". Do not say "I finally realize how much I love you" or anything that has a negative connotation.
7. If she has left, do not ask her to come back. You can do that later, just not now. Do not ask questions like, "Why did you leave? What did I do wrong?" Such questions have negative connotations and tend to also bring emotional pressure on the other person. Rather ask questions like: Did you know you are the greatest lover?
8. Do not talk about forgiveness yet. The strategy is to reconnect with your wife's heart through what she was designed to crave the most – LOVE.
9. During the next thirty days, DO NOT ask your wife for anything. This is strictly a time of building up, stirring up and fixing your relationship.

## How it Works

1. Decide on what time of the day you will send your text messages. It is important that you send you text messages at the same time everyday.

2. Communicate your message (via text message only). The strategy in this book has worked very well with text messages, and we do not yet know how much effective other avenues are.

3. After sending your message, write your present moment thoughts, and feelings.

4. Use this book as your diary: Write down any responses you receive, lessons learned, any other experiences you might have gone through and anything you deem important.

5. If it helps, discuss with your friends about your activities, however, please watch out for negative friends, especially the ones that always find something negative to say about her. I strongly suggest that you stay away from friends of the opposite sex unless they are family.

6. When you send your text messages, send them as they are written in this book. Do not add a 'period' or full stop at the end of the message. Trust me, it makes a huge difference.

7. Extra help for those who desire to save and improve their marriage is available at TovNation@Gmail.com. Please only seek extra help after you have used this book for at least 10 days.

**Let's Get Started...**

I love you

I love you more everyday

# I love you

I'm thinking about you right now

# You are beautiful

You're so smart

I love you

I value your insight

# Just thinking about you makes me feel good

I really admire your inner strength

I'm one lucky man because I have you as a friend

I have loads of love for you

I love you

On the agenda for tonight: me loving you

You're one of the most interesting people I've ever met

I'm so grateful to have you in my life

# I'm thinking of you

I hope you are having a great day

# Thank you for being a friend

I love you

I'm so thankful that we fell in love with each other

# Good morning beautiful

# I'm so thankful that we met

# Thinking about your smile

# I love our life together

I love you

Just smiling and thinking of you

You smell really good

I love you

You are beautiful

**Well done for completing 30 days of loving and reconnecting with your spouse.**

How is it going for you? Is this strategy working well for you? If yes, please feel free continue loving and reconnecting with him. Nothing beats intimate connection between spouses!

If you have done everything by the book and not much improvement has come your way, and you could do with extra help, contact TovNation@Gmail.com immediately.

My desire is to help you save and improve your marriage.

I appreciate you so much

# I love being with you

I love you

I love you

Thank you for being you

# You're the best person

I love us

Thank you for being a beautiful wife

# I'm glad you're my friend

I love you

# You're a good wife

# I really appreciate you

You are awesome

I love you so much

Thank you for working so hard

# You're an excellent person

I love you

# You're so smart

# You're amazing

# You're so strong

You're a hard worker

# I feel happy with you

# I like you

# I love you

# You're so considerate

# You're a great lover

# I'll enjoy being with you

I'm blessed you are my wife

# You are a godly woman

# Thank you

**Well done for completing 60 days of loving and reconnecting with your spouse.**

How is it going for you? Is this strategy working well for you? If yes, please feel free continue loving and reconnecting with him. Nothing beats intimate connection between spouses!

If you have done everything by the book and not much improvement has come your way, and you could do with extra help, contact TovNation@Gmail.com immediately.

My desire is to help you save and improve your marriage.

I love you

It's fun to be married to you

# You are a generous person

You are my favorite person in the entire world

# I want to grow old with you

You're trustworthy

# I trust your intuition

I love you

# You are a thoughtful woman

# I have confidence in you

I love you

I totally trust you

# I'm proud to be your husband

# There's no one like you

You stand for the truth. I admire that

I love you

# You are a woman of faith

# You are a woman of integrity

You're amazing – you really are

# You're a woman of action

I love you

You're simply the best

I love you

Thank you for being a faithful wife (and mother)

# The heavens must really be looking out for me to give me you

# You are a woman of excellence

# You're a beautiful lady

I love just being with you

I'll love you always and forever

I love you

No matter what level of disconnection and pain your marital relationship is currently experiencing, your marriage can be saved, improved and be a happy one. Extra help for those who desire to save and improve their marriage is available at
TovNation@Gmail.com

Made in United States
Orlando, FL
10 August 2024